bush
PUBLISHING
& associates

DREAMS to DIRECT YOU

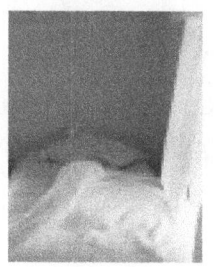

By Ivy Harrison

Unless otherwise indicated, all scripture quotations in this resource are from the *King James Version* of the Bible.

Scripture quotations marked AMPLIFIED are taken from *The Amplified Bible*, Old Testament copyright © 1965, 1987 by Zondervan Corporation, Grand Rapids, Michigan. The Amplified New Testament copyright © 1958, 1987 by the Lockman Foundation, La Habra, California. Used by permission.

DREAMS to DIRECT YOU
Copyright © 2008 by Ivy Harrison
All Rights Reserved
Printed in the USA
ISBN: 978-0692481585

All rights reserved. Reproduction of contents and/or cover in whole or part without written permission is prohibited.

Cover Design by Margo Bush
Bush Publishing & Associates
Tulsa, Oklahoma

Printed in the United States of America

Table of Contents

About the Author … 7
Special Thanks … 9
Preface … 11
Chapter 1: Introduction … 13
Chapter 2: Purpose of Dreams … 17
Chapter 3: Biblical Dreamers … 21
Chapter 4: Dreams and ELECTRICAL ACTIVITY OF THE BRAIN … 25
Chapter 5: Interpretation of Dreams … 29
Chapter 6: Personal Examples … 33
Chapter 7: Dreams on Angels … 39
Chapter 8: Conclusions … 45
References … 49
For More Information … 51

About the Author...

Elder Ivy Harrison founded and Pastors Spread the Word Ministries of Laurel, Inc. In addition to Pastoring, Pastor Harrison serves as Mathematical Statistician for the Department of Transportation in Washington, DC. She holds a Masters in Religious Education from the Washington Saturday College, a Masters in Statistics from Florida State University, and a B.S. in Mathematics from North Carolina A&T State University. Pastor Harrison is married to Elder Dennis Harrison and they have two children Christina (Richard) and Dennis, Jr., and one grandson, Reid. They currently reside in Laurel, Maryland.

Special Thanks...

A special thanks to Dr. Larry Williams and Dr. Joan B. Sanders for their encouragement for me to complete this book.

This book is dedicated to my parents:
The late Minnie Hawkins Moody
and the late Glen Moody

Preface...

By Ivy Harrison

> "If there be a prophet among you, I the Lord will make myself known unto him in a vision, and will speak unto him in a **dream**. My servant, Moses... with him will I speak mouth to mouth...."- Num. 12:6-8

Vision for 2000 and Beyond: In order to accomplish things for God in the 21st century we must learn how to effectively communicate with God. This book will examine the ways God communicates with His people as mentioned in Num. 12:6-8, mainly dreams, visions, and mouth to mouth. Communication for humans normally involves two people talking to each other. But in addition to verbal communication there is also non-verbal communication, which involves not only what is said but also nonverbal things such as facial expressions and hand movements.

Prayer is the main way we communicate with God. The major way God communicates with us is through His written Word, visions, dreams, or by speaking to us. Also God can reveal things to us through the use of our mind. This happens when God gives us revelation as to what a scripture or some other event means. Other revelation gifts in scripture involve a Word of Knowledge, a Word of Wisdom, or Discerning of Spirits, which God supernaturally reveals to bless or deliver a person.

Volume I will address Dreams to Direct You and Volume II will address Visions and other Revelation Gifts. The Word says where there is no vision the people perish.

CHAPTER 1

Introduction

"If there be a prophet among you, I the Lord will make myself known unto him in a vision, and will speak unto him in a dream. My servant, Moses, is not so, who is faithful in all mine house. With him will I speak mouth to mouth...." - Numbers 12:6-8

In the Old Testament a prophet or prophetess was a man or woman of God who received messages direct from God to give to a group of persons or an individual. Our theme scripture in Numbers chapter 12 relate the three main ways God spoke to His servants which include the following ways: 1) visions, 2) dreams, 3) mouth to mouth. The focus of this book is how God uses dreams to speak to His people.

Natural Dreaming: All of us have experienced dreaming at some point. More details will be given on natural dreaming in Chapter 4 as many researchers have studied this topic.

Biblical or Prophetic Dreaming: The word dream is found in 13 books of the Bible. In the Old Testament the word chalom (khalome) means dream (-er). In the New Testament the word enupnion (en-oopl-nee-on) means something seen in sleep, i.e. a dream (vision in a dream).

Moses is the only person in scripture that God elected to speak mouth to mouth with as stated in Numbers 12:8. In Exodus 33:11 it is recorded that the Lord spoke unto Moses *"as a man speaketh unto his friend."* This was prior to God writing the Ten Commandments on tables of stones for a second time. God also spoke mouth to mouth with Adam and Eve in the Garden of Eden.

The major prophets were used to God revealing himself to them through visions and dreams. Such prophets as Isaiah and Ezekiel, God spoke to mainly through the use of visions. With a vision a person is often shown a picture while being awake. In Acts 10:11 Peter saw a vision of a great sheet with all manner of four-footed beasts being received into heaven. This is when God let Peter know what God has cleansed call not common and the Gentiles received salvation through faith and Peter preached at Cornelius house.

In the Old Testament God spoke to the prophet Daniel and Joseph, God often revealed himself to them through the use of dreams. Daniel's dreams often dealt with future world events whereas Joseph's dreams dealt with events in his life. In addition both of these men were known for their ability to interpret dreams. The revelation of the meaning of a particular dream was often given to them as they sought God in prayer and fasting (See Daniel 2 and Gen 41:15-16).

In this book we see how God speaks to his servants through the use of dreams. God revealed himself to Joseph through the use of a dream in Gen 37:9 where the sun and the moon and the eleven stars made obeisance to Joseph. The significance of this dream was seen later in Joseph's life.

A much quoted scripture in both the Old and New Testament involving dreams is Joel 2:28 and Acts 2:17 which states: "In the last days your sons and daughters shall prophesy, your old men shall dream dreams, your young men shall see visions." Again we see three ways God speaks: prophesy (from God's mouth to prophet's mouth), dreams, and visions. Old in this verse refers to old, aged, ancient, elder(-est).

In the New Testament Ephesians 4:11 talks about the five-fold ministry gifts which include: apostle, prophet, evangelist, pastor, and teacher. These gifts are given for the perfecting of the saints, for the work of ministry, and for the edifying of the body of Christ. Anyone operating in one of these ministry gifts should understand how God communicates with His people. A better understanding of how God communicates should enable a person to function more effectively in any of the ministry gifts.

CHAPTER 2

Purpose of Dreams

Dreams have been defined as thoughts visualized in sleep or movies in your mind. In Chapter 1 we saw that dreams in addition to being thoughts visualized in sleep, represent one of the major ways God speaks to his prophets and servants. Since dreams are used by God to communicate with us we need to understand their purpose. In scripture we see five major purposes for dreams, which include:

(1) Warnings (restraint from evil)

(2) Revelation of God's Will

(3) Encouragement

(4) Revelation of the Future

(5) Direction or Instruction

Next Biblical examples of dreams that were used for each of the above five purposes will be given.

(1) Warnings (Gen 20:3-7): When Abraham went to Gerar, he told Abimelech who was the King of Gerar, that Sarah was his sister and he did not reveal that she was also his wife. As a result Abimelech took Sarah but God intervened on Sarah's behalf. *"But God came to Abimelech in a dream by night, and said to him, Behold, thou art but a dead man, for the woman whom thou hast taken; for she is a man's wife. ...And God said unto him in a dream, Yea, I know that thou didst this in the integrity of thy heart; for I also withheld thee from sinning against me: therefore allowed I thee not to touch her. Now therefore restore the man his wife; for he is a prophet, ... and thou shalt live: and if thou restore her not, know thou that thou shalt surely die, thou, and all that are thine."*

(2) Revelation of God's Will (Gen 28:11-22)- In Genesis 28 Jacob dreamed about a ladder reaching heaven. God revealed His will to Jacob that He would give him and his seed the land he was laying on. In his seed God promised to bless all the families of the earth. This is a confirmation of the Abrahamic Covenant to Jacob.

(3) Encouragement (Judges 7:13-15) – When Gideon had selected his army according to God's instructions he ended up with 300 warriors to fight against the Midianites. *"When Gideon was come, behold, there was a man who told a dream unto his fellow, and said, Behold, I dreamed a dream, and, lo, a cake of barley bread tumbled into the host of Midian, and came unto a tent, and smote it that it fell, and overturned it, that the tent lay flat. And his fellow answered and said, This is nothing else except the sword of Gideon, the son of Joash, a man of Israel; for into his hand hath God delivered Midian, and all the host."- Judg. 7:13-14* When Gideon heard the dream and its interpretation he was so encouraged that he worshiped and told the host of Israel to arise for the Lord hath delivered into your hand the host of Midian.

(4) Revelation of the Future (Gen 37:5-10) – The first dream Joseph dreamed in Genesis 37 was that he and his brethren were binding sheaves in the field, and Joseph's sheaf stood upright and his brethrens' sheaves made obesisance to Joseph's sheaf (Gen 37:7). He dreamed a second dream that was similar to the first in which the sun and the moon and the eleven stars made obesisance to Joseph. These dreams revealed Joseph's future place of authority over his family in which he was used to save the lives of his family and others as he was placed in charge of food distribution during a time of great famine.

(5) Direction or Instruction (Matt. 1:20) - Joseph (Mary's husband) was directed in a dream to take Mary as his wife as the child she had conceived was of the Holy Ghost. While Joseph thought on the events of the day an angel appeared unto him in a dream and gave him clear direction.

CHAPTER 3

Biblical Dreamers

There are very few students of the Bible who have not heard of two famous dreamers in scripture both with the name Joseph. The first dreamer named Joseph appears in the first book of the Old Testament and the second dreamer named Joseph appears in the first book of the New Testament. Let's take a look at both of these dreamers.

Old Testament Joseph: The twelve tribes of Israel equates to the twelve sons of Jacob. Altogether Jacob had twelve sons by four different women. The two sons by the wife Rachel, whom he loved, were Joseph and Benjamin. Rachel dies once she delivers Benjamin. It is Jacob and Rachel's son Joseph that is the Old Testament dreamer. When Joseph was 17 years old, his father gave him a coat of many colors. Joseph dreamed a dream found in Gen 37:9 – *"And he dreamed yet another dream, and told it his brethren, and said, Behold, I have dreamed a dream more; and, behold, the sun and the moon and the eleven stars made obeisance to me."*

His father's response to his dream was: *"shall I and thy mother instead come to bow down ourselves to thee to the earth?"* His father observed the saying but his brothers disliked him for his dreams and also because they felt like their father favored him over them. Joseph was placed in a pit by his brothers, went to prison, but ended up in the palace where he became prime minister over Egypt and was in charge of food distribution. In Gen 50:18 we see his brothers bowing before him: *"And his brethren also went and fell down before his face; and they said, Behold, we be thy servants."* So initially it did not appear as if Joseph's dream had any significance. When he became prime minister of Egypt and his entire family had to come before him to receive food, the dream truly revealed the future about Joseph and his family.

New Testament Joseph: Our New Testament dreamer is Mary's espoused husband Joseph. At Christmas and other times we often discuss how the angel appeared to the mother of Jesus, Mary, but often we forget that an angel also appeared to Jesus earthly father Joseph in a dream. In Matt 1:19-20 we have an account of this dream: *"Joseph her husband, being a just man ... while he thought on these things, behold, the angel of the Lord appeared unto him in a dream, ... fear not to take unto thee Mary thy wife."* Here we clearly see that God is no respecter of persons. He revealed to both parents that Jesus was a special child that they were being selected to raise.

As the child grew, God continued to speak to Joseph in dreams. Matt 2 records another important time that God spoke to Joseph through a dream. In Matt 2:12-13 *"And being warned of God in a dream that they should not return to Herod, ... the angel of the Lord appeareth to Joseph in a dream, ... take the young child and his mother and flee to Egypt."* By Joseph following the instructions given to him by the angel from God: the life of Jesus was spared.

CHAPTER 4

Dreams and ELECTRICAL ACTIVITY OF THE BRAIN[1]

The brain is not an electric machine which runs on electricity but it is a biochemical machine that runs on metabolic substances. Nevertheless, the electricity generated as a byproduct of the electrochemical events can be measured and the measurements so obtained permit scientists to examine the more basic electro-chemistry. A physician doesn't open the chest to observe the heart but relies upon listening to the heart sounds with a stethoscope. He has learned that the various sounds signify different events and conditions. Analogously, the brain scientist does not open the brain but relies on an **electroencephalogram** (EEG) to record the electrical activity in the brain and the underlying electrochemical events.

There are two ways to record the electrical activity of the brain. The first and most common is to place metal disc electrodes on the surface of the scalp and record

---

[1] *A Primer of Psychobiology* (Brain and Behavior) by Timothy J. Teyler, 1975, WH Freeman and Company.

the electrical activity of the brain beneath. The very weak signals are amplified and recorded on a moving paper. The graphic record is an **electroencephalogram (EEG)**. Figure 1 (diagram shown on page 39) shows a schematic of the recording instrument, which is called an electroencephalograph—see Figures at the end of the book. Electrodes can be placed over many different brain areas and an EEG can then be made of the activity of countless millions of brain cells acting, more or less, together.

To the uninitiated the EEG appears to be a meaningless collection of squiggly lines. However, study reveals consistent patterns in EEGs and relationships between certain patterns and various behavioral states. The most profound changes in EEG take place as a person progresses from the fully awake, alert state into deep sleep. The EEG of an awake, alert person is characterized by a general lack of "waves," the activity being slight, rapid, and irregular as shown in Figure 2(diagram shown on page 39). During relaxed wakefulness the dominant wave frequency recorded on an EEG is between eight and twelve oscillations per second. This is termed **alpha activity.** The EEG of a sleeping subject is characterized by large, slow waves (Fig. 2). If we observed a subject's EEG throughout a night we would notice periods in which it looked just as it did during alert wakefulness. This phenomenon puzzled brain scientists, who named it paradoxical sleep because the subject is sleeping but his brain waves resemble those of an alert, awake person. When subjects were awakened during this period of paradoxical sleep, they reported that they had been in the throes of a dream. **Thus, the EEG made while the subject is dreaming resembles that of an awake individual!** Observation revealed that the eyes dart to and fro during dreams, giving rise to the term rapid-eye-movement **(REM)** sleep to describe the dreaming state.

Apparently we all dream, although some of us are better at recalling dreams than others. Experiments have shown that even persons who claim they "never dream" actually do, although not as often as other people. They apparently forget the dreams they do have. The "average dreamer" has five to seven per night with each dream lasting from 10 to 40 minutes. Dreams get longer as the night progresses (Fig. 3–shown on page 40). Contrary to popular belief, we dream in "real time," not in super-fast or super-slow time. Many people dream in color and stereophonic sound! Most of us are unaware of the subject matter of most of our dreams. We generally remember a dream best if we are awakened in the midst of it. In detailed studies of dream content, hundreds of people were queried about the contents of thousands of dreams. The picture that emerges is that novelty has a predominant role in dreams. A third of dream time is spent merely in going away from or toward something. A high proportion of dream time is taken up by active sports and a low proportion by dull routine. People report that the dreams following a rather dull day are sometimes spectacular and exciting, whereas the dreams following a day full of invigorating activities tend to be bland and tame. It is almost as if a dream were compensating for daily activity.

REM sleep is not limited to adults; it has been observed in newborn infants and many animals. A sleeping dog or cat can be observed to move his eyes rapidly, perhaps move his limbs, and vocalize. The animal is exhibiting that it is in REM sleep, and although we cannot confirm it, is almost certainly dreaming. The obvious question is, "What does a newborn baby or a dog dream about?" Unfortunately, we cannot answer this question directly.

In summary, the electrical activity of the brain can be detected by two means. Surface recording of brain activity, which produces the EEG, has shown us that patterns of brain activity change dramatically as a person moves from one to another of the different states of wakefulness and sleep. Studies of EEGs of sleeping subjects have shown the somewhat surprising fact that when a person is dreaming his EEG resembles that recorded during alert wakefulness. Periods of dreaming are associated with rapid eye movements (REM) in many species. Other behavioral state produces characteristic EEG patterns. An example is the alpha wave associated with relaxed wakefulness. A technique for studying brain activity, which is generally not used in humans, is the recording of brain activity from electrodes inserted directly into the tissues of the central nervous system.

Experiments using this technique have provided us with much information regarding brain mechanisms underlying sensation, perception, and action.

CHAPTER 5

Interpretation of Dreams

In Daniel Chapter 2, King Nebuchadnezzar dreamed a dream that troubled him but he could not remember the dream. He told the magicians, astrologers, sorcerers, and Chaldeans to make known the dream and the interpretation of the dream otherwise the king would have them cut into pieces. If they reveal the dream and its interpretation the king promised to give them gifts, rewards, and great honor. The Chaldeans tried to get the king to tell them the dream because they had not been given such a hard request as they were used to interpreting revealed dreams only. The Chaldeans said there is not a man alive that can do what the king had requested.

They sought Daniel and his fellows to be slain with the other wise men. Daniel requested of the king that he would give him time, and that he would show the king the interpretation. Daniel went to his house and prayed to God along with his companions Shadrach, Meshach, and Abednego, that God would reveal the king's secret. The king's dream was revealed to Daniel after they prayed in a night vision or dream. Daniel had an excellent spirit within himself that was a gift from God to interpret dreams. Daniel was often given the interpretation to dreams as he sought God in prayer or meditated on the dreams. At other times his dreams were interpreted for him as part of the dream. God would use an angel or a person in the form of a man in the dream to give Daniel the interpretation of the dream.

After Daniel interpreted King Nebuchadnezzar's dream, the king told Daniel that his God was a God of gods and a revealer of secrets seeing thou couldest reveal this secret. The king made Daniel ruler over Babylon and over the other wise men and gave him great gifts. Daniel requested that his friends in prayer Shadrach, Meshach, and Abednego, be placed over the affairs of Babylon and Daniel sat in the gate of the king.

In Genesis Chapter 41 Pharaoh dreamed two dreams that were similar where seven ears of corn came up upon one stalk that was fat. Then seven thin ears of corn came and devoured the seven fat ears. Pharaoh called for all the magicians of Egypt and told them his dreams but there were none that could interpret his dreams.

Pharaoh heard from his chief butler that Joseph could understand a dream to interpret it. Similarly, Joseph's gift, like Daniel's gift, was given to him because the Spirit of God was in him. Joseph let Pharaoh know that God would give the interpretation to his dreams. Joseph told Pharaoh that his two dreams were one and that God had revealed to Pharaoh what he was about to do. The dream was given twice because the thing was established by God and that God would shortly bring it to pass. The dream meant there would be seven years of plenty followed by seven years of famine. Joseph was put in charge of all the land of Egypt and was second only to Pharaoh. Joseph was in charge of storing food doing the good years to prepare for the years of famine. Pharaoh put his ring on Joseph's finger, arrayed Joseph in fine linen and put a gold chain about his neck. Joseph and Daniel both were promoted as a result of their gift from God to interpret dreams. The scriptures let us know that your gift will make room for you.

CHAPTER 6

Personal Examples

Next I will give examples of dreams that I have had. These dreams will be described in general without revealing names to protect the identity of persons involved. I will relate the dreams I have had to the five major purposes for dreams discussed earlier.

(1) Warnings:

Dream 1 - In this dream I was talking to a friend late at night over the phone and her husband came to the phone and he was weeping so hard he could not speak. I shared this dream with my friend and as we meditated on the dream I told my friend I felt this could represent the passing of her husband's grandmother who was sick at the time. Her husband had been raised by this grandmother so her husband went to visit his grandmother on Thursday and his grandmother passed on that Friday. My friend called me late that Friday night to say her husband's grandmother had passed. When she called late at night it was as if I was reliving my dream. I had the feeling that God had warned us in time for my friend's husband to be able to say goodbye to his grandmother. But I also felt like I had been given a snap shot of the future before it came to pass. God is an all knowing God.

Dream 2 - Once I dreamed my boss on my job stopped me by the mailboxes and said you got to move after saying his boss was on a warpath. The next week my co-worker who shared an office with me and I were both informed by our team leaders that we were moving. The scriptures let us know that God will allow nothing to come on us unaware. The Lord warned us about the move before our bosses informed us of their plan. Events like this caused me to become aware that often dreams are used to warn us about certain events before they happen.

Dream 3 (Feet from House to House) Once I dreamed about a man's feet going from house to house. I recognized the feet to be that of a friend's boyfriend. I believe this was a warning about my friend's boyfriend being unfaithful to her. When people are in love it is hard for them to receive warnings because sometimes they want the person more than they want to know the truth. I find God sends warnings especially if certain events will cause a particular person a great deal of pain. Events later in life proved that God was trying to warn my friend of great hardship that would be caused to her by this boyfriend's unfaithfulness. The Spirit of God knows the hidden things of the heart.

(2) Reveal God's Will:

Dream 4 - After working several years on one job I started looking for another job. I wanted to know whether to continue working where I was or to accept one of the several job offers that would allow me to use my background in statistics. I dreamed I pulled a statistics book (Blue in color) written by Hogg and Craig on Mathematical Statistics off a shelf. I remember using this book in graduate school and I still had a copy of this book. To me this was an indication that God's will for me was to accept one of the positions in statistics. Once I got on the new job I used the Hogg and Craig book to answer certain statistical questions and it reminded me of my dream.

Dream 5 - After signing a contract to purchase a new home I wondered if it was God's will for my family to make this move. I had a dream about a big yellow Ryder truck being in our driveway. To me this was a clear indication that it was time for us to move. We rented our old house and moved into an apartment while we waited for the new house to be built. It was very difficult securing a moving truck as we were not aware that you need to make reservations way in advance for these trucks especially during certain times of the year. The only truck my husband was able to get was a yellow Ryder truck. As I saw the truck in our driveway I knew our steps were being ordered by God.

(3) Encourage:

Dream 6 - One dream I had was about a teacher making negative marks on one of my children's papers. In the dream the Spirit encouraged us not to receive the negative report. As I meditated on the dream the Lord let me know that I was not to receive the negative report my child's teacher was giving us about my child's ability to read. As the result of us not receiving the report our child became an honor roll student instead of being dyslectic as the teacher was suggesting. Thank God for his directions in a difficult situation.

(4) Reveal Future

Dream 7 - Once I dreamed about two persons being stabbed in the heart. One person being stabbed was my aunt and one was my mom. This dream turned out to be symbolic of future events of my aunt's close cousin being stabbed by her boyfriend and my mom's close friend having a massive heart attack.

Dream 8 - I dreamed about one of my friend's boyfriends announcing his marriage intentions to my friend. Many times it looked like they would not marry but in the end they did get married. Truly the Spirit sees and reveals future events.

Dream 9 - Once a close friend stopped talking to me and years later I dreamed she started talking to me again. Sure enough after having gall bladder surgery this friend called me and started talking to me.

(5) Directions or Instructions

Dream 10 - Once I dreamed I walked in a room and someone tried to give me a package with a bomb in it. The instructions from this dream was not to receive negative words because they are like a bomb that will cause you to explode.

Dream 11 - I dreamed about having jealous feelings toward a certain person. The instruction was to remove jealousy from my life. Dream 6 is also an example of a dream where instruction and encouragement was given.

CHAPTER 7

Dreams on Angels

In Luke16 it discusses when the beggar Lazarus died and Angels came and carried him into the arms of Abraham's bosom. Read the text below. In this chapter I will describe two dreams I recently had on Angels.

Luk 16:19   There was a certain rich man, which was clothed in purple and fine linen, and fared sumptuously every day:

Luk 16:20   And there was a certain beggar named Lazarus, which was laid at his gate, full of sores,

Luk 16:21   And desiring to be fed with the crumbs which fell from the rich man's table: moreover the dogs came and licked his sores.

Luk 16:22   And it came to pass, that the beggar died, and was carried by the angels into Abraham's bosom: the rich man also died, and was buried;

Luk 16:23   And in hell he lift up his eyes, being in torments, and seeth Abraham afar off, and Lazarus in his bosom.

Dream One on Angels: The first dream I had on Angels reminded me of the tv show *Touched By An Angel*. In the dream I was sitting in my sunroom at home and two angels that appeared as ladies one black and one white was in the dream. So in this first dream the angels appeared as people. I was about to have an heart attack and the Angels told me to just relax- it reminded me of when you have surgery and the medication helps you to relax before surgery. Transitioning to heaven can be as relaxing as having medication before surgery. In the dream I was fine until the two Angels pointed at me as if they were coming to take me to heaven.

All I could say was what about my children. My children are not ready for me to go to heaven. When I woke up the next morning I was very happy to be in the land of the living. As a result of this dream I sought the Lord for the meaning of the dream. The revelation that was given to me was that we all have a certain number of days upon the earth but that God can grant us an extension. In the Old Testament Hezekiah was granted 15 years when he turned his face to the wall and prayed unto God. (Read 2 Kings 20:1-7 below)

2Ki 20:1	In those days was Hezekiah sick unto death. And the prophet Isaiah the son of Amoz came to him, and said unto him, Thus saith the LORD, Set thine house in order; for thou shalt die, and not live.
2Ki 20:2	Then he turned his face to the wall, and prayed unto the LORD, saying,

2Ki 20:3	I beseech thee, O LORD, remember now how I have walked before thee in truth and with a perfect heart, and have done *that which is* good in thy sight. And Hezekiah wept sore.
2Ki 20:4	And it came to pass, afore Isaiah was gone out into the middle court, that the word of the LORD came to him, saying,
2Ki 20:5	Turn again, and tell Hezekiah the captain of my people, Thus saith the LORD, the God of David thy father, I have heard thy prayer, I have seen thy tears: behold, I will heal thee: on the third day thou shalt go up unto the house of the LORD.
2Ki 20:6	And I will add unto thy days fifteen years; and I will deliver thee and this city out of the hand of the king of Assyria; and I will defend this city for mine own sake, and for my servant David's sake.
2Ki 20:7	And Isaiah said, Take a lump of figs. And they took and laid *it* on the boil, and he recovered.

Dream Two on Angels: The second dream I had on Angels was on Winged Angels. In the second dream on Angels I could hear the Wing of the Angel moving. I was wrestling with the winged Angel and I said release me and I will witness to all about Christ. This dream occurred early in the morning and disturbed me to the point I woke my husband as I could not go back to sleep. I woke my husband to tell him about the dream. I believe the significance of this dream is that our focus needs to be on soul winning.

In addition I think the significance of these dreams is that God wants us to know that His Word is true and everything in His word is true including Angels. Also I believe God wants us to better understand as Christians as to what happens when we die so that we do not have to fear death as Christ conquered death. The Word says to be absent in the body is to be present with the Lord. In addition if we read Luke 16:24-31 listed below it describes a gulf that separates the dead from the living and that living has to hear the Word from the living as once people go to heaven they cannot return to warn their love ones. Also it describes place of torment where those go that do not believe in Christ.

Luk 16:24   And he cried and said, Father Abraham, have mercy on me, and send Lazarus, that he may dip the tip of his finger in water, and cool my tongue; for I am tormented in this flame.

Luk 16:25   But Abraham said, Son, remember that thou in thy lifetime receivedst thy good things, and likewise Lazarus evil things: but now he is comforted, and thou art tormented.

Luk 16:26	And beside all this, between us and you there is a great gulf fixed: so that they which would pass from hence to you cannot; neither can they pass to us, that *would come* from thence.
Luk 16:27	Then he said, I pray thee therefore, father, that thou wouldest send him to my father's house:
Luk 16:28	For I have five brethren; that he may testify unto them, lest they also come into this place of torment.
Luk 16:29	Abraham saith unto him, They have Moses and the prophets; let them hear them.
Luk 16:30	And he said, Nay, father Abraham: but if one went unto them from the dead, they will repent.
Luk 16:31	And he said unto him, If they hear not Moses and the prophets, neither will they be persuaded, though one rose from the dead.

The **Authorized Version** or **King James Version (KJV)**, 1611, 1769.

CHAPTER 8

Conclusions

What should we do when we have dreams? First determine if it is a natural or spiritual dream? If it is a spiritual dream maintain a healthy relationship with God, keep a journal, pray about it and ask God to reveal the meaning of the dream. Also it is important to seek God for whether the dream is symbolic or literal. Finally seek God on whether to share your dream with a particular person. Remember, Joseph's family became jealous when he revealed his dreams.

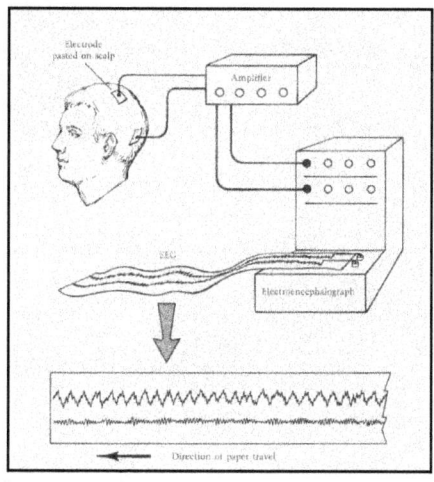

Figure 1

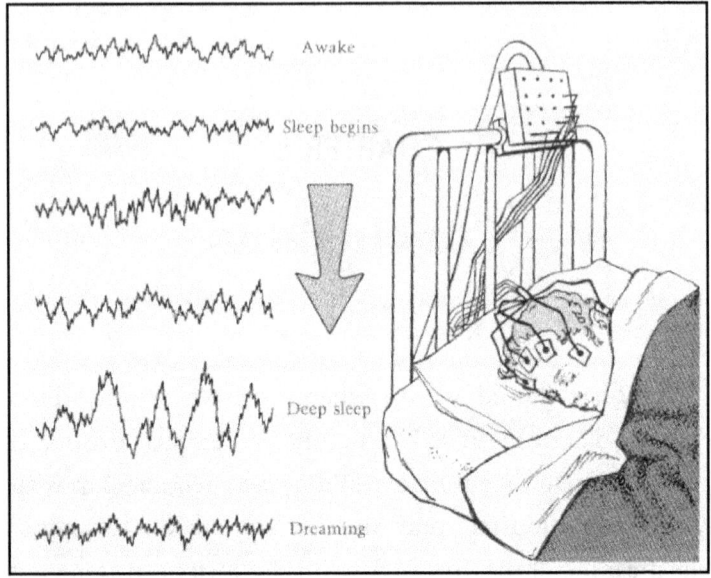

Figure 2 Typical EEGs from subjects in different states ranging from alert wakefulness to dreaming.

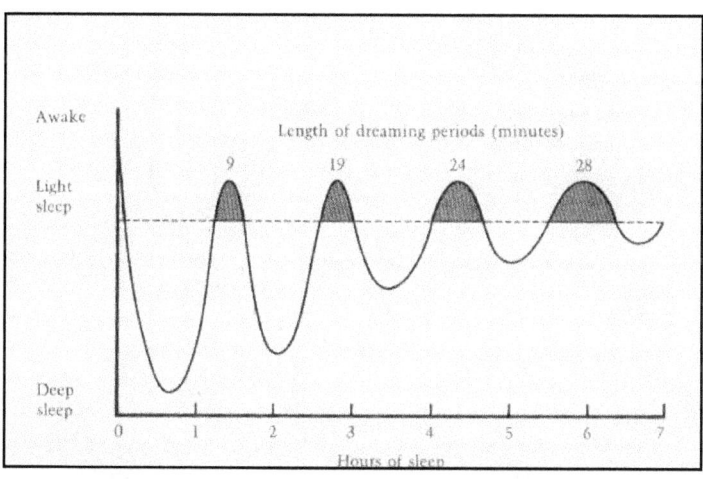

Figure 3 A typical night of sleep-darkened areas indicate periods of dreaming. The depth of sleep progressively declines toward morning and the length of the dreaming periods increases.

References

King James Version of the Bible

A Primer of Psychobiology (Brain and Behavior) by Timothy J. Teyler, 1975, W H Freeman and Company.

For More Information

For more information regarding additional copies of this book and others by Rev. Ivy Harrison please write or call:

Rev. Ivy Harrison
Spread the Word Ministries of Laurel, Inc.
9055 C Maier Road
Laurel, Md. 20707
301-490-1741
spreadthewordministries.net

www.ingramcontent.com/pod-product-compliance
Lightning Source LLC
Chambersburg PA
CBHW061301040426
42444CB00010B/2467